PEGASUS ENCYCLOPEDIA LIBRARY

Experiments and Activities
PHYSICS

Edited by: Aparna Chatterji
Managing editor: Tapasi De
Designed by: Vijesh Chahal and Anil Kumar
Illustrated by: Suman S. Roy, Tanoy Choudhury
Colouring done by: Vinay Kumar, Sonu, Kiran Kumari & Pradeep Kumar

PHYSICS

CONTENTS

Introduction	3
Which falls faster?	4
Plasticine and coins	5
Making a spray jet	6
Black and white	7
Creating multiple images of an object	8
Finding the centre of gravity	9
Properties of light	10
Convex mirrors and convex lenses	11
Vary the tone	12
Pictures of your voice	13
Singing bottles	14
Tolling bells	15
A hovering paper clip	16
Electricity and magnets	17
Electricity in your hair	18
Dancing under glass	19
Reflection of sound	20
Working of a camera	21
Merging colours	22
Mysterious mirror	23
Ribbons show airflow	24
Expanding a balloon	25
Can metal be extended?	26
Does air have any weight?	27
Fountains at home	28
Lightning from a spoon	29
What absorbs more heat?	30
A flying ping pong ball	31
Index	32

Introduction

Learning and experiencing new things is a continuous process. Children are much more inquisitive than we elders are. They are always bubbling with enthusiasm when it comes to knowing new things. That is the reason they are so full of questions. This enthusiasm should never be curbed; instead, it should be encouraged!

It is a proven fact that children learn the most by doing, experiencing and seeing things. Teaching them through books and worksheets only, does not suffice. We all know that 'seeing is believing'.

But sometimes due to the constraint of time and many other factors, elders are not successful in giving those experiences and exposure to their children which they deserve.

This encyclopedia on Physics helps the young readers to understand their surroundings better. It is full of experiments and activities that give knowledge about the common things of life like light, sound, air, gravity and the numerous other things that a child should know in order to cope up with his surroundings better. This series can be a proud possession of any child who is interested to enhance his practical knowledge.

Which falls faster?

The fact

Two objects of varying size and weight would hit the ground at the same time when dropped from the same height, provided there is no air resistance.

What will happen?

In the first case the metal plate will reach the floor first, and in the second they will arrive together.

What you need

- A metal plate
- A paper plate

How to do the experiment?

1. Hold both the plates horizontally. Let them fall at the same time.
2. Now place the metal plate over the paper plate and let them fall together.

Conclusion

The metal plate and the paper both fall under the influence of the Earth's gravitational force, but in the first case the metal plate falls faster than the paper plate as it has a higher mass per surface area. The paper plate has lower mass per surface area due to which the resistance from air slows down its fall to a greater extent as compared to the metal plate.

In the second case the metal plate and the paper plate encounter the same resistance; hence, they hit the ground at the same time.

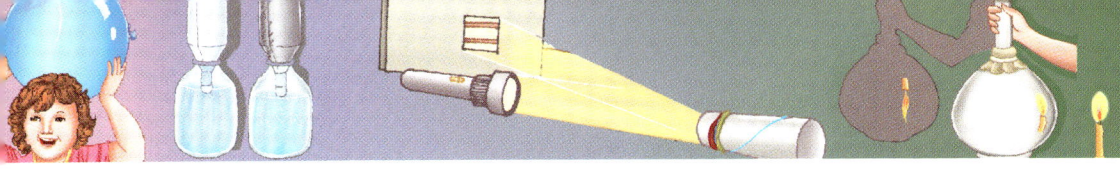

Plasticine and coins

What you need

- Two identical coins
- A plasticine lump

How to do the experiment?

1. Place one coin (horizontally) on the plasticine and press it down with your finger.

2. Now place the other coin on the plasticine sideways (vertically) on its edge and repeat the experiment.

What will happen?

The second coin (one which is placed vertically) will sink into the plasticine much deeper than the first. Plasticine, is a type of modelling clay, a putty-like modelling material made from calcium salts, petroleum jelly and aliphatic acids.

Conclusion

The area of contact of the second coin with the plasticine was much lesser than that of the first. So, the pressure it exerted was also higher and so it sank deeper into the plasticine than the first coin.

Making a spray jet

The fact

An atomizer is a device which converts a stream of liquid into a fine spray. Atomizers mix air with the liquid via a pumping mechanism.

What you need

- A plastic drinking straw
- A glass of water
- A penknife

How to do the experiment?

1. Cut the straw half-way along one third its length.
2. Bend the straw as shown.
3. Immerse the shorter end into the glass and make sure the cut is above the level of the water.
4. Blow air hard through the free end.

What will happen?

Water will enter the straw from the glass and will then be expelled through the slit as a spray.

Conclusion

The strong current of air you have made by blowing reduces the pressure at the top of the immersed part of the straw. The normal pressure acting on the water is now stronger than this reduced pressure, and it forces the water to flow up. The moving air blows the water off in drops.

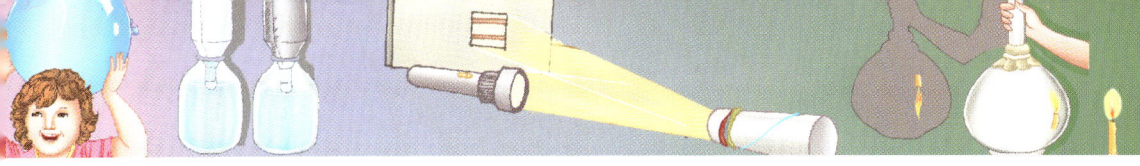

Black and white

The fact

This experiment will tell you that heat reaches objects through radiation.

What you need

- Two identical bottles
- Two identical glass jars
- Water
- Two pieces of paper, one white and one black of identical size and thickness

How to do the experiment?

1. Wrap white paper around one bottle and black paper around the other.
2. Dip their openings into the jars which you have filled with water (as shown).
3. Put both into direct sunlight.

What will happen?

More bubbles of air will be streaming out of the bottle wrapped with black paper.

Conclusion

Black absorbs more radiated heat than white, and the air in the bottle with the black paper will be heated more than that in the other bottle. As it expands, it tries to escape from the bottle.

Now, put the bottles along with the jars in a cool place. Soon you will see that more water has gone into the bottle with the black paper, proving that more air had been displaced from it.

PHYSICS

Creating multiple images of an object

The fact

Multiple images can be produced by using two plane mirrors. As the angle between the mirrors decreases, the number of images that can be seen increases.

What you need

- Two books
- Two book-sized plane mirrors
- Two rubber bands
- A pencil

How to do the experiment?

1. Use the rubber bands to fix the mirrors to the books.
2. Place the books upright with the mirrors facing each other.
3. Place the pencil between the books as shown.
4. Look into one mirror and try to see what you can.

What will happen?

You will see numerous images of the pencil on both the mirrors!

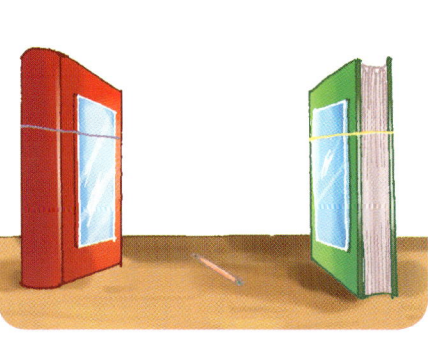

Conclusion

The light rays from the pencil bounce many times from one mirror to the other before they reach your eyes.

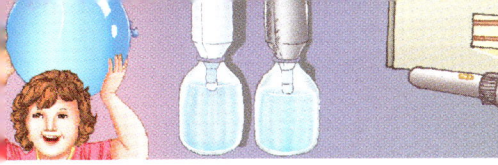

Finding the centre of gravity

The fact

Centre of gravity of an object is the average location of its weight. Let's find out the centre of gravity of a few things through simple experiments.

What you need

- A book
- A broom
- A ruler
- Other objects

How to do the experiment?

1. Balance a book on your index finger, helping yourself with your other hand until you find the spot where you can easily balance the book horizontally.

2. Hold the broomstick horizontally on both your outstretched index fingers. Slowly move the fingers towards each other, until they meet at the broom's centre of gravity.

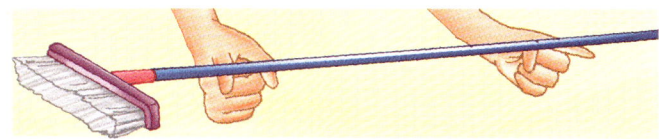

3. Try and balance the broom vertically on your forehead.

4. Try various other objects and find their state of equilibrium.

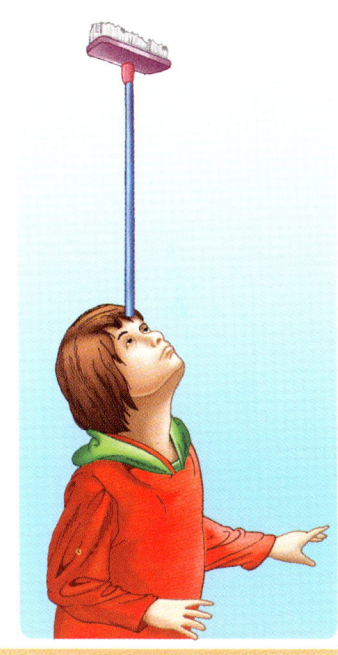

Conclusion

The centre of gravity is an imaginary point about which all the weight (mass) has been evenly distributed in an object. Whenever the centre of gravity lies directly over the base of support, the object remains perfectly balanced and steady.

Properties of light

The fact

Rays of light travel at a great speed in a straight line. When they touch our eyes, they convey to us a lot of information about the things around us. This experiment will show just this.

What you need

- Two pieces of cardboard
- A candle
- A pencil
- A ruler
- A sharp cutter

How to do the experiment?

1. Cut out slits vertically on the cardboard pieces and set them up as shown.
2. Make the candle stand right in front of the slit of one of the cardboards. Now light the candle.
3. Now try to see the candle and its flame through the slits of the cardboards.

What will happen?

The flame will be visible to your eye.

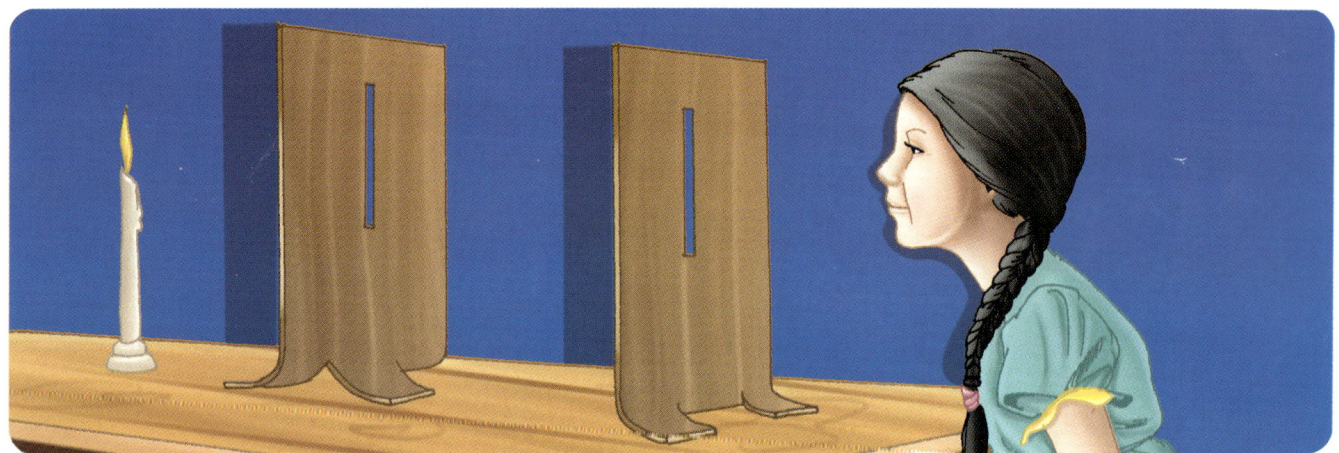

Conclusion

When the candle, both the slits on the cardboards and your eye are in a straight line, only then will the flame of the candle be visible. This is due to the fact that light travels along a straight line.

Convex mirrors and convex lenses

The fact

Images are formed when light rays coming from an object get reflected by a mirror or when they pass through a lens.

What you need

- A spherical glass bottle
- A candle
- Water

How to do the experiment?

1. Fill the bottle with water and hold it between a burning candle and the wall.
2. Keep moving the bottle until you get a sharp image.

What will happen?

You will see a miniature image of the candle on the bottle, while a inverted and magnified image will appear on the wall.

Conclusion

The outer surface of the bottle acts as a convex mirror, which reflects the reduced images of objects. The water in the bottle acts as a convex lens, which produces a inverted and magnified image on the wall.

Vary the tone

The fact

The pitch of the sound produced by a wire depends on its thickness, length and how tightly it is stretched.

What will happen?

Every change of tension of the wire or distance will produce a different tone.

What you need

- A steel wire
- Two buckets of water,
- Two thin wooden strips

How to do the experiment?

1. Place the strips of wood on a table.
2. Stretch the wire across the strips and tie its ends to the two buckets.
3. Change the tension of the wire by adding water to the buckets and also change the distance between the strips. Pluck the wire.

Conclusion

As the distance between the strips is increased, the length of the wire increases and low pitched sounds are produced. However, the pitch of sound made by the wire does not entirely depend on its length. It also depends on how tightly it is stretched (the tension of the wire). An increase in the tension of the wire produces a corresponding increase in the pitch.

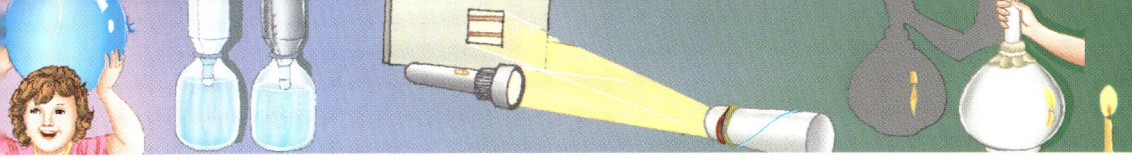

Pictures of your voice

The fact

If you want to see a picture of your voice, try the following experiment.

What you need

- A balloon
- Scissors
- A short cardboard tube
- A rubber band
- Some metal foil
- A flashlight
- Glue

How to do the experiment?

1. Stretch a piece of the balloon rubber tightly across one end of the tube and fix it with the rubber band.
2. Stick a small piece of foil on the balloon rubber.
3. Switch on the flashlight and position it as shown, so that it is pointing at the metal foil at an angle enabling you to see a spot of light reflected on a wall or a piece of paper.
4. Say something into the open end of the tube, changing the pitch and loudness of your voice.

What will happen?

Dashes and wavy lines will appear on the spot of light!

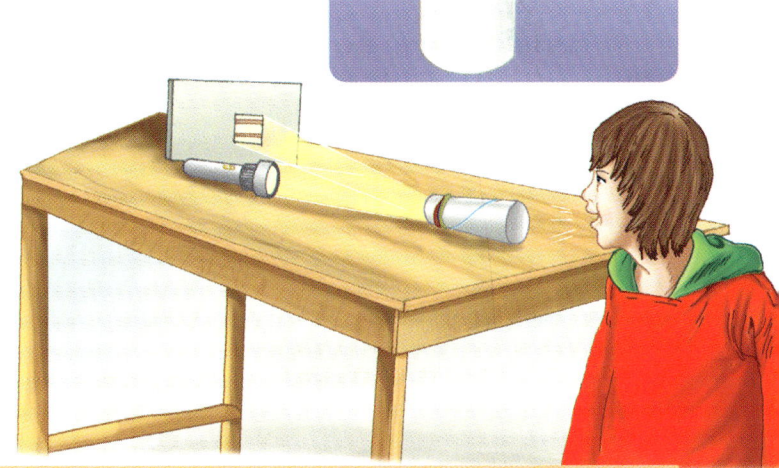

Conclusion

The vibration of your voice makes the air in the tube vibrate. This forces the balloon, foil and therefore also the reflected light to vibrate. You will be able to see this in the form of short lines and wavy lines in the spot of light.

Singing bottles

The fact

This experiment will show how sound energy can be transferred from one vibrating object to another.

What you need

- Two identical bottles

How to do the experiment?

1. Place the top of a bottle next to your ear.
2. Your friend should stand about one metre away from you and blow across the top of his bottle.

What will happen?

You will hear from your bottle a tone of the same pitch as that coming from the other bottle.

Conclusion

The air vibrations in one bottle induce vibrations in the other, creating a tone of the same pitch but somewhat of lower intensity. This phenomenon is called resonance.

Tolling bells

The fact

The source of sound is typically any vibrating matter. The vibrations then travel away from the source through any medium such as air.

Through this experiment, we will produce a sound that will remind you of tolling bells.

What you need

- A piece of string one metre long
- A fork

How to do the experiment?

1. Tie the fork to the string as shown in the picture.
2. Wind the two ends a few times around your index fingers and put your fingers in your ears.
3. Swing the fork so that it hits a hard object.

What will happen?

You will hear a sound like the tolling of bells.

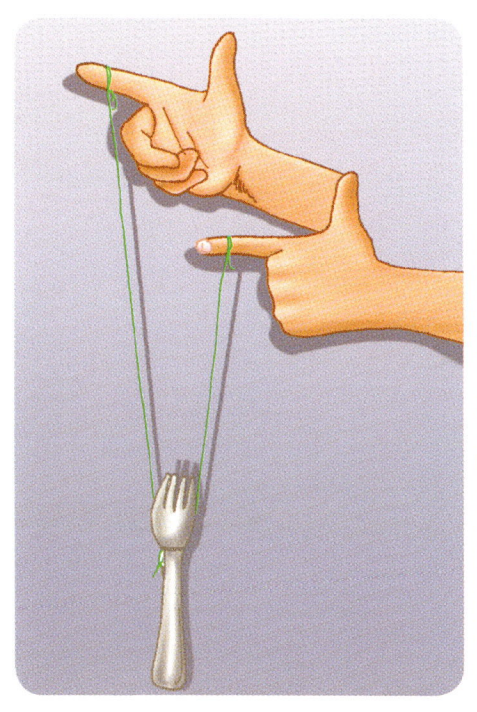

Conclusion

As the fork hits another object, it begins to oscillate. The vibrations are conveyed through the string and your fingers straight to your ear drums.

15

PHYSICS

A hovering paper clip

The fact

Magnets attract certain types of stainless steel objects too. Stainless steel is an alloy of iron which contains other metals like chromium or nickel. If the steel sample contains only chromium in the mix, then the steel sample would not exhibit magnetic qualities.

What you need

- A steel paper clip (not containing nickel)
- Thread
- Adhesive tape
- A magnet

How to do the experiment?

1. Tie the paper clip to one end of the thread and tape the other end of the thread to the surface of the table.
2. Slowly bring the magnet close to the paper clip.

What will happen?

With a little practice, you will be able to make the clip dance like a cobra.

Conclusion

Stainless steel objects that do not contain nickel are also attracted to magnets.

Electricity and magnets

The fact

Electricity and magnetism have a deep relation. Through this experiment let us show you how. A wire carrying electric current generates a magnetic field around itself.

How to do the experiment?

1. Let the magnetized needle float in the water and tape the wire over it in the same direction in which it is pointing.
2. As soon as you link the wire to a battery, the needle will turn, showing that the conductor through which the electricity is running also acts as a magnet.

What you need

- A magnetized needle on a piece of cork
- A thin wire
- Adhesive tape
- A plateful of water
- An electric battery

Conclusion

As soon as the wire is connected to the battery, electric current starts flowing through it. This generates a magnetic field around the wire which interacts with the magnetic field of the magnetized needle and causes it to turn.

PHYSICS

Electricity in your hair

The fact

Static electricity can be produced by rubbing two different materials, specially non metals.

Here is an experiment in which you can use your own hair to make static electricity.

What you need

- String
- Two balloons
- Adhesive tape

How to do the experiment?

1. Stick the string with tape over the two balloons so they are about five to six centimetres apart.
2. Rub one of the balloons on your hair and let it hang next to the other balloon.

What will happen?

The balloons will first attract each other but once they touch they will repel each other.

A step further

Tear a paper tissue into tiny pieces. Rub a balloon on your hair and bring it close to the paper bits, which will then fly up and stick to the balloon.

Conclusion

Rubbing the first balloon with hair caused it to attain negative static charge. Thus, the charged balloon attracted the second balloon which was neutral. However, when the balloons came in contact with each other, charge transfer took place which caused both the balloons to attain negative charge. Hence, the second balloon was repelled.

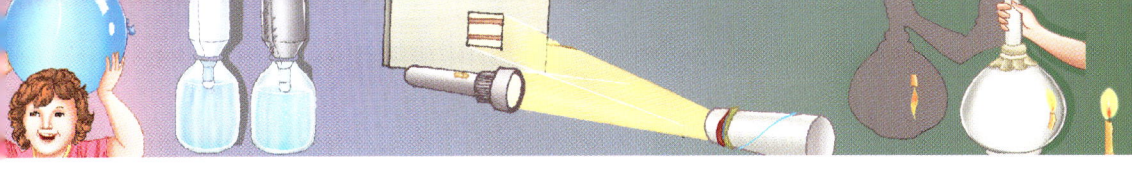

Dancing under glass

The fact

Let us make a puppet theatre which uses static electricity.

What will happen?

The little men will begin to dance up and down.

What you need

- A piece of glass
- A metal tray
- Aluminium foil
- A silk cloth
- Several large books

How to do the experiment?

1. Cut out several human figures from the foil and place them on the tray.
2. Place 4 books at the 4 corners of the tray and place the glass on top.
3. Rub the glass with the silk cloth. Be careful not to break the glass.

Conclusion

Rubbing the glass with cloth charges the glass with static electricity. The charged glass then attracts the figures, to which the charge is then passed. Equal charges repel each other, so the figures then fall off the glass and on to the tray, to which they pass their charges, and then they are attracted up to the glass again.

Reflection of sound

The fact

Sound can be reflected from a wall as light from a mirror. Let us see how this happens through this experiment.

What you need

- Old newspapers
- Scissors
- Adhesive tape
- A wind-up clock
- A broomstick

How to do the experiment?

1. Twist a newspaper page tightly around the broomstick. Tape the paper and pull the tube off the stick.
2. Make another tube in similar manner.
3. Hold one tube at an angle towards the wall and place the clock at its end, as shown in the picture.
4. Your friend should point the other tube at the wall and place his or her ear at its end, as shown in the picture.

What will happen?

Your friend will hear the clock clearly.

A step further

Experiment with different positions of the tubes and see how sound is reflected.

Conclusion

The sound waves emitted by the clock travel through the first tube, and strike the wall. The waves are then reflected from the wall and enter the second tube, which carries them to your friend's ear making it possible for him or her to hear the clock ticking.

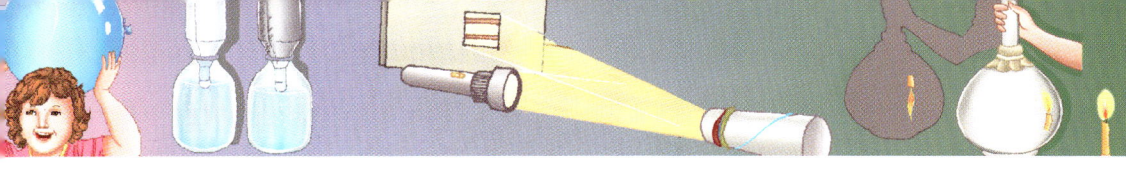

Working of a camera

The fact

A camera is a box which can form an image on a photographic film or on other light-sensitive medium.

What you need

- A small box properly sealed for light
- Translucent paper
- Scissors
- A pin
- Adhesive tape

How to do the experiment?

1. Cut out one of the sides of the box.
2. Replace the missing side with the translucent paper and fix with the tape. Stretch the paper well before fixing it.
3. Make a small hole with the pin in the centre of the side opposite to the translucent paper.
4. Hold up the box with the hole towards a window and move it back and forth slowly.

What will happen?

You will see an upside-down image of the window.

Warning!

1. The camera works best when you aim it at a brightly lit object.
2. In order to be able to see the image displayed on the translucent paper, you need to block out any ambient light. So, it would be advisable to drape an opaque blanket over your head and the camera.

Conclusion

We already know that light travels in a straight line. The rays from the window pass through the hole and hit the paper. Those from the bottom will, therefore, hit the top edge of the paper and those from the top the bottom edge. So, what you will see will be an inverted image of the window.

Merging colours

The fact

The colour white is a mixture of all the colours. Let us prove this through this experiment.

What you need

- A pencil
- A compass
- Thick white paper
- Scissors
- Paints

How to do the experiment?

1. Make a circle on white paper and cut it out.
2. Divide the circle into segments of equal sizes and paint them with all the colours of a rainbow.
3. Make a small hole in the centre of the circle and pierce it with a pencil.
4. Spin it as fast as you can.

What will happen?

All the colours will merge. If you have painted it with all the colours of a rainbow, the colour you see when you spin the circles will be white.

Note: In case you are unable to observe white colour, you need to spin the wheel faster. You can attach the wheel to a simple motor to make it spin faster.

A step further

Take three flashlights and cover the bulbs with red, blue and green cellophane. In a darkened room, point them at a white wall or a piece of paper. Let the rays mix. How many new colours have you produced?

Conclusion

The circle spins so fast that our eyes cannot see the individual colours but only a mixture of all the colours. White is a mixture of all the colours. So, the colour which will be visible to you will be white.

Mysterious mirror

The fact

A mirror image is not an exact copy of the people and things facing the mirror. Let us check.

What you need

- A mirror
- A pencil and some paper

How to do the experiment?

1. Make a drawing of your choice and write its subject underneath.
2. Hold the mirror and your drawing upright against each other.
3. Look at the reflection of your drawing and the letters in the mirror.

What will happen?

The mirror image will be laterally inverted. So will the letters and you may not be able to read your inscription.

A step further

Make 2 mirrors stand facing each other. Keep a small object between them. Look at the mirrors and you will see an endless row of images on both the mirrors.

Conclusion

Rays of light travel in a straight direction unless they hit an obstacle from which they reflect. Light from the sun, a candle's flame and electric bulbs hits our eyes directly, but we see most other things with the help of the light from other sources which hits those things and is then reflected to our eyes.

Polished surfaces such as mirrors reflect light very well. But when you look at yourself in a mirror, you see the left side of the face on the right and the right side on the left. The face you see in the mirror is not the same face others see when they look at you directly. The same goes for other objects, except that you can compare their mirror images with the originals, but you cannot do so with your own face.

Ribbons show airflow

The fact

Heat energy is transmitted in the form of airflow. Let us see how through this experiment.

What you need

- Thin sheets of paper
- Adhesive tape
- Scissors
- A warm room and a cool room next to it

How to do the experiment?

1. Cut long ribbons from the paper.
2. Stick one end of the ribbons along the top and bottom edge of a door.
3. Open the door slightly.

What will happen?

The ribbons will fly in the opposite directions. The ones at the top of the door will fly from the warm room towards the cold room and the ones at the bottom from the cold room to the warm one.

A step further

Stick a ribbon half-way up the door. Will it move?

Conclusion

Warm air is lighter than cold air and always rises to the upper part of the room. As you open a door, it streams out causing the ribbons at the top to fly towards the cold room. On the other hand, cold air streams into the warm room to replace the warm air through the lower end of the doorway. This causes the ribbons at the bottom to fly towards the warm room.

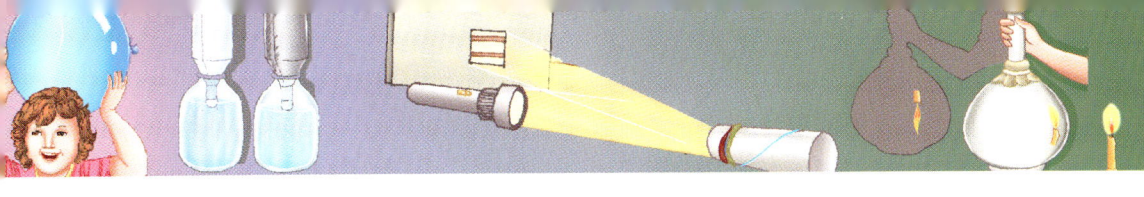

Expanding a balloon

The fact

Gases expand on heating. The size of the balloon can be increased without blowing air into it. Let's check how.

What will happen?

The balloon will gradually expand until it bursts.

What you need

- A balloon
- A candle

How to do the experiment?

1. Place the balloon next to a burning candle and watch what happens.

Conclusion

The air molecules move faster and faster under the influence of heat and the air present inside the balloon expands until the balloon bursts.

25

Can metal be extended?

The fact

We know that solids expand when heated. Let us see how.

What you need

- Two bottles
- A cork stopper
- A long aluminium knitting needle
- A sewing needle
- A candle
- A piece of paper
- Scissors

How to do the experiment?

1. Stick the knitting needle into the cork with which you have already plugged one of the bottles.
2. Place the other end of the needle across the top of the other bottle as shown in the picture.
3. Make a paper arrow and pierce it with the sewing needle in the middle.
4. Place the needle with the arrow on top of the bottle which does not have the cork on top.
5. Heat the knitting needle with the candle.

What will happen?

The paper arrow will rotate as you heat the knitting needle.

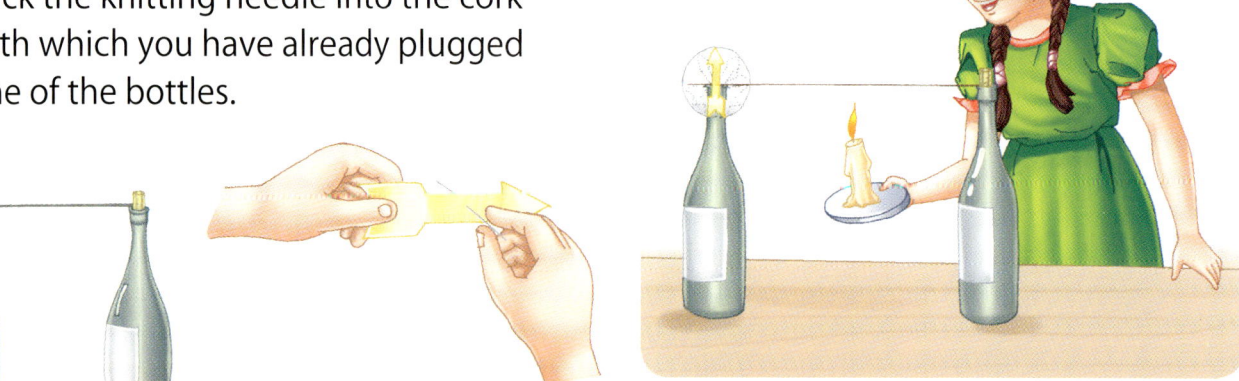

Conclusion

The knitting needle expands and gets longer due to the heat thus it turns the sewing needle, rotating the arrow as well.

Does air have any weight?

The fact

It is true that air has weight and exerts pressure on the objects with which it is in contact. This simple experiment will prove it.

What will happen?

The water will stay in the glass and the cardboard will not fall off.

What you need

- A glass of water
- A piece of smooth shiny and firm cardboard

How to do the experiment?

1. Cover the glass of water with the cardboard. Holding the cardboard against the rim of the glass, carefully turn it upside down.
2. Slowly remove your hand.

Conclusion

This happens because air exerts its pressure from all directions. Its upward pressure against the cardboard is sufficient to keep the water in the glass.

PHYSICS

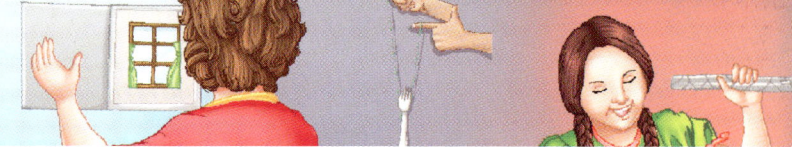

Fountains at home

The fact

A liquid's weight produces hydrostatic pressure, which acts in all directions. Let us show this through this experiment.

What you need

- Two plastic bags
- A pin
- Water

How to do the experiment?

1. Fill the bags with water and seal them.
2. Holding in the position shown in the picture, pierce with the pin at several places.

What will happen?

The water will flow out in different directions as the hydrostatic pressure acts on it.

Note: To help your experiment succeed, you should also pierce the water bag at the top, so that the atmospheric pressure can also act on the water.

Conclusion

Hydrostatic pressure causes the water to flow out.

Lightning from a spoon

The fact

Lightning takes place due to transfer of charge from the clouds to the Earth. Let's perform a simple experiment to observe how this transfer takes place.

What you need

- Three dry glasses
- A metal tray
- A plastic ruler
- A metal spoon
- woollen cloth

How to do the experiment?

1. Place the glasses next to each other as shown.
2. Place the tray on top of them.
3. Charge the ruler by rubbing it with the cloth and put it on top of the tray.
4. Hold the spoon close to the tray.

What will happen?

There will be an electric spark like the lightning between the tray and the spoon.

Conclusion

The electricity from the ruler flows into the tray and then jumps from it to the spoon in the form of lightning.

What absorbs more heat?

The fact

When you're out in the sun on a hot summer day it is better to wear some light coloured clothes as they absorb less heat. Dark colours absorb more heat. Let us prove this through this simple experiment.

What you need

- 2 identical drinking glasses or jars
- Water
- Thermometer
- 2 elastic bands or some sellotape
- White paper
- Black paper

How to do the experiment?

1. Wrap the white paper around one of the glasses using an elastic band or sellotape to hold it on.
2. Do the same with the black paper to the other glass.
3. Fill the glasses with equal amount of water.
4. Leave the glasses out in the sun for a couple of hours before returning to measure the temperature of the water in each.

What will happen?

The glass wrapped in black paper absorbs more light and heat than the one wrapped in white paper. Measuring the temperatures of the water will show that the water in the black paper wrapped glass was hotter than the other glass. Lighter surfaces reflect more light, that's why people wear lighter coloured clothes in summer so that it keeps them cooler.

Conclusion

Dark coloured objects absorb more heat as compared to light coloured objects.

A flying ping pong ball

The fact

Gravity and air pressure play an important role. Let us show how through this simple experiment.

What you need

- At least 1 ping pong ball (2 or 3 would be great)
- A hair dryer

How to do the experiment?

1. Plug in the hair dryer and turn it on.
2. Put it on the highest setting and point it upwards.
3. Place your ping pong ball above the hair dryer and see what happens.

What will happen?

Your ping pong ball floats gently above the hair dryer without shifting sideways or flying away. The airflow from the hair dryer pushes the ping pong ball upwards until its upward force equals the force of gravity pushing down on it. When it reaches this point it gently floats where the upward and the downward forces are equal.

A step further

Try floating 2 or even 3 ping pong balls as an extra challenge.

Conclusion

Two equal and opposite forces cancel out the effect of each other.

Index

A

air resistance 4
atomizer 6

C

centre of gravity 9
charge 18, 19, 29
chromium 16
convex lens 11
convex mirror 11

E

electric battery 17
equilibrium 9
expand 25, 26

H

horizontally 4, 5, 9
hydrostatic pressure 28

I

inverted image 21

L

lightning 29

M

magnified 11
molecules 25

N

nickel 16

P

phenomenon 14
photographic film 21
pitch 12, 13, 14
pressure 5, 6, 27, 28, 31

R

radiated heat 7
resonance 14

S

sound waves 20
static charge 18
surface area 4

V

vibration 13